The Next Big Asian Brands

THE NEXT BIG

ASIAN BRANDS

Jörg Dietzel

Published in 2022 by Marshall Cavendish Business
An imprint of Marshall Cavendish International

Other Marshall Cavendish Offices:
Marshall Cavendish Corporation, 800 Westchester Ave, Suite N-641, Rye Brook, NY 10573, USA • Marshall Cavendish International (Thailand) Co Ltd, 253 Asoke, 16th Floor, Sukhumvit 21 Road, Klongtoey Nua, Wattana, Bangkok 10110, Thailand • Marshall Cavendish (Malaysia) Sdn Bhd, Times Subang, Lot 46, Subang Hi-Tech Industrial Park, Batu Tiga, 40000 Shah Alam, Selangor Darul Ehsan, Malaysia

National Library Board, Singapore Cataloguing in Publication Data
Name(s): Dietzel, Jörg, 1961-
Title: The next big Asian brands / Jörg Dietzel.
Description: Singapore : Marshall Cavendish Business, 2022.
Identifier(s): ISBN 978-981-5009-64-4 (paperback)
Subject(s): LCSH: Brand name products--Asia--Management. | Branding (Marketing)--Asia.
Classification: DDC 658.827095--dc23

Printed in Singapore

CONTENTS

PREFACE

THE IDEA WAS CLEAR: to look at brands that originated in the region, but not those that have been looked at numerous times by many authors. Instead, I wanted new brands that were up-and-coming.

But that's more easily said than done. The brands couldn't be too big and known already, otherwise they're "now", not "next". On the other hand, they couldn't be too small and obscure because in that case they'd be hard to find and there'd be no guarantee that they'd make it big. (There's never a guarantee – bigger brands also fail, but initial momentum can give us a good idea of the potential they have.) And forget trying to find them if you're not in the market.

So I reached out to friends, colleagues, business partners, former students in the region – from India to Indonesia, Japan to Korea, China to Singapore, Vietnam, Thailand. Who did they see as the up-and-coming brands in their region or industry?

From a long list, I homed in on the brands you see in this book. They represent the most exciting brands over diverse geographies and industries, ranging from food (pizza to cakes) to cosmetics, an online marketplace to e-mobility, manscaping solutions to career guidance.

Oh yes, and Covid. When I started working on this book, the world was in the middle of the pandemic. Which led me to the question: How – apart from making their life and work difficult – has Covid impacted these brands, forced them to pivot in the way they produce, sell, communicate?

What can we learn from their success strategies, and will these learnings still be relevant long after the pandemic is over?

The insights and learnings generated surprised me, and I had to admire the resilience of every single brand I spoke to, all of whom used the pandemic to redouble their efforts, rethink their business model, and restructure their offer to make it relevant in an unprecedented global crisis.

I have let the brands speak for themselves in this book. In many cases, you will hear directly from the founders, whose responses vividly capture the thrill of steering their startups to success – as well as the sometimes painful lessons learnt along the way.

You will also find thematic summaries throughout the book, where I distil key takeaways and action points.

Every brand here inspires in its own way, and I watch their growth with great anticipation. I hope you will similarly find their stories insightful – whether for your own brand or for brands that you may work for/with.

It Started With a Cut

BOVEM

SINGAPORE

Manscaping – especially when it comes to trimming below the waist – just isn't a topic you bring up casually in Asia. Enter BOVEM, whose line of precision-grade tools leads the charge in overcoming this taboo, on its way to bringing safe and stylish male grooming to the world.

Even before he attended my Advertising class, I got to know Lydon Ong as a young creative – he participated in international advertising competitions and (together with Max Ang) won awards against big agencies, doing Singapore Management University (SMU) proud.

Then, on a panel for the SMU Incubator, I faced him and Norman Teo online as they presented their BOVEM idea.

The idea of manscaping is relatively new. Males seem to always lag behind females when it comes to grooming, and it took Japan and Korea to come out with specific skincare, shampoos and even decorative cosmetics aimed at men.

Slowly, this made a male skincare regime more acceptable – even through many brands are still fighting the notion that it is somehow “unmanly” to take care of yourself and convince the many males who use their wives’ shower gels and shampoos to get their own.

Male grooming took even longer to be accepted, and to this day the taboo about trimming body hair, wherever it may be, exists.

Secretly, most of us have trimmed “down there” before, using a pair of scissors and our electric shaver. Not ideal. It was only recently that male grooming gear popped up around the world, looking to overcome the taboo by taking on a very masculine positioning, tongue-in-cheek communication and videos of rambutans being shaven!

BOVEM is a good example for this trend, born out of personal experiences.

Interviewees
Lydon Ong and Norman Teo, Co-Founders

SECOND EDITION
Manscaping
Redefined
BOVEM GLOBE TRIMMER 2.0
BOVEM

Share with us a little about the beginnings of your brand. What gave you the initial push? What was the gap and opportunity you saw in the market?

"Some years ago, while trying to groom below the waist, I experienced a bad cut while navigating the hard-to-reach regions with my scissors and razor. After that accident, I thought to myself, there must be a better way to do this. I shared this with Norman, and that was the genesis of BOVEM.

"Through our research, we found that more than 50% of Asian males groom below the waist regularly. But just like me, many often turn to tools like a pair of scissors or their facial razor to do so. Without proper tools available in the market, this was our impetus to establish our position as the first-mover in the Asian market."

Did you recognise a trend or consumer insight that you could tap into?

"Below-the-waist grooming is generally still considered a private topic in Asia and is in its early stages of adoption, without much conversation surrounding it.

"However, these perceptions are shifting as more Asian men become more in tune with their body, motivating them to adopt better grooming methods.

"We believe that this proliferation could arise from imported Western grooming habits, especially driven by social platforms such as Instagram, YouTube and TikTok, where these influences are prominent.

"BOVEM aims to tap into the growing personal grooming space in Asia and provide precision-grade grooming tools for men to properly groom 'down under'."

How do you differentiate your brand from the other players in your segment?

"We position and brand ourselves differently from our competitors. BOVEM takes on a witty, quirky, yet classy persona on our social platforms such as TikTok, which are powerful tools that enable us to stay relevant to the millennials and Gen Zs.

"Unlike the traditional players that focus on marketing the product, BOVEM strives to find a balance between doing so and building rapport with customers on an individual level – to be a friend more than a brand.

"By using these virality-driven social platforms to evoke emotions, we are able to amass a following and a long-term word-of-mouth ecosystem that serves as a lasting marketing strategy."

How would you define your target group? Do you differentiate your message to appeal to different needs?

"The majority of our audience belong to millennials and Gen Zs aged between 21 and 34 years old. This is the age group that has experience in personal grooming, albeit not a routine set in stone. They also tend to be open to experimenting with different personal care products that can enhance their lifestyle.

"At the moment, we've found success by focusing on humour, educating about wellness, and being self-improvement-oriented. Humour creates a space that allows men to be vulnerable and have conversations that are typically uncomfortable. Through that lens, we see men being more receptive to our messaging around wellness education and self-improvement."

When building your brand, what was the biggest hurdle you faced and how did you overcome it?

"The first year of starting the business was the toughest as we didn't have anything built in yet and no structured processes in place. It was a slow, painstaking process to create the BOVEM that we know today. There are many aspects to consider, and so much thought has to be put into what seems simple and sometimes unnoticeable for the end user.

"Working in a team and trusting each other has allowed us to work more efficiently and get the right support that we need.

"One challenge was thinking of a fitting messaging for an intimate product, one that wouldn't come off as 'rude' or 'cheap'. We had to find the right balance of wit, playfulness and elegance, without overstepping into the cheesy, in-your-face territory. We also wanted to make sure to tie our brand back to modern elements, to maintain the classy look of our brand.

"In the early stages, we tested different messaging and branding angles with small audiences. This really helped us to see what sticks with our audience and aligns with our overarching brand image."

One way to create something new is to disrupt convention. What are you disrupting and how?

"Ultimately, we are disrupting the taboo around below-the-waist grooming and intimate grooming by extension.

"For many years, the men's grooming market mainly focused on facial and head products. But as consumers become conversant with grooming 'down under', exploring alternate grooming habits, and looking for more ways to enhance their grooming journey, they uncovered the need for grooming with the right tools on different parts of the body."

BOVEM

How do you keep track of changing consumer preferences and behaviour that could impact your brand?

"From the early stages, we instituted an effective feedback loop, and inculcated the practice of listening to every review, complaint and feedback. This allows us to be accountable to our customers and their feedback, for example on product and packaging changes, leading to business improvements.

"As the brand grows, this support component remains vital for gathering insights and as a foundation to understand what customers care about and prefer.

"We also actively conduct social listening on the different platforms to monitor trends and conversations surrounding the industry. Every week, our team will come together to share insights and trends that we discover online. This allows us to uncover opportunities and channels that BOVEM could hop on.

"This way, we are up-to-date on the latest news and in-the-loop about any changing consumer preferences."

How has Covid-19 impacted your business?

"BOVEM is a business born out of the pandemic. The height of the pandemic coincided with our university summer break, which gave us the time to deep-dive into building the brand. Much of the business conceptualisation and initial building was done at a time when the world was getting used to teleconferencing, and we telecommuted the months leading up to our launch.

"In a way, we sometimes think that the business might not have started if we were not privileged with extra time on our hands to build BOVEM!

"The pandemic has accelerated certain trends that have been visible for several years. We believe that e-commerce and digital advertising will continue to grow as consumers continue to shop online more after the pandemic. We want to position BOVEM well to enjoy that shift in consumer behaviour."

Can your brand stretch and extend into other segments? Any plans?

"We plan to move beyond focusing our efforts mainly on Asia, to expand strategically in other geographies where men pride themselves on being refined, with more targeted marketing efforts as well as planned distribution channels.

"We also hope to horizontally expand beyond the groin to serve the broader grooming market over time and provide a more diversified range of products to improve men's grooming routines."

Where do you see your brand in five to ten years' time, in terms of business offer, geography, target groups?

"We envision BOVEM to be the market leader in innovative men's grooming and to have our products available worldwide, with Asia being the main geographical market."

LESSONS FROM COVID

- **E-commerce is here to stay. Think about channels and create convenience.**

- **Customers are individuals. Each one is special. Look at them as friends.**

- **Use downtime to rethink your process.**

- **Focus on digital channels for communication and brand-building.**

SO YOU WANT TO START A BRAND? #1

The Idea

AT A RECENT guest lecture at Stellenbosch University Business School in South Africa, the MBA Head told me that these days, given the state of the South African economy, most MBA students would not get jobs with the big consultancies as before. Instead, they'd have to pivot and find a different role – or start their own brand.

So I wasn't too surprised when after my talk (on the Experience Economy), a young female MBA student came to me and told me that she had plans to start her own fashion brand after graduation.

"That's great," I said. "So how is it different?" That's the question you're most likely to hear from me.

"Oh, it's sustainable," she replied. "The fabrics, the dyes, the way I treat my staff..."

"Good," I said. "But that's probably not enough. Being sustainable in fashion is important, maybe a necessary fact when you want to appeal to Gen Zs, but I don't think it's enough. Nobody buys a piece of fashion just because it's sustainable. It needs to look good. Once you crack the design, *and* you're sustainable, you have a good chance to succeed in the market."

Of course you'd start with an idea. You want to change the world, disrupt whatever industry you've chosen to be in. And everything is built on that idea.

But will that idea work? The fact that nobody has tried it before could be an opportunity to fill a gap. Or there could be a good reason why nobody has done this and succeeded – maybe it's just not something people want. So check your idea to make sure it's relevant, differentiated and consistent.

Good for Your Skin

BATH & BLOOM

THAILAND

Bath & Bloom is success story in "mass luxury" skincare, whose customers value natural ingredients, thoughtful design and sustainable – and are happy to pay a premium for it. Born in Thailand, the ambitious brand is poised to take on the world.

Sometimes it takes a little longer for a trend to become global.

Anita Roddick founded The Body Shop on 27 March 1976 in Brighton, UK, almost 50 years ago. And while successful, the idea of using natural ingredients and recyclable containers took a while to spread to the mass market.

BATH&BLOOM
THAI JASMINE
BODY LOTION
BATH&BLOOM
THAI JASMINE
CONDITIONER
BATH&BLOOM
BATH&BLOOM
THAI JASMINE
HAND CREAM
THAI JASMINE
BODY SCRUB

Until very recently, China required animal testing as an entry condition for cosmetics into their huge market, and for decades brands emphasised the effects of their cosmetics rather than the ingredients.

But slowly the tide changed. With a growing global awareness of sustainability, millennials and now Gen Zs started asking brands questions about their values: where do they source their ingredients, how natural are they, and how do they treat their staff, their producers, the environment?

With more awareness of the side effects of chemicals came the preparedness to pay a bit more for natural ingredients that are gentle on the skin.

At the top end of the market, brands like Aesop combined natural ingredients with minimalist design and created a successful natural skincare and haircare brand, together with fragrances, candles and accessories. At the lower end of the market, more affordable brands like Lush appealed to a younger demographic through storytelling and a more fun retail experience.

In between, there's Bath & Bloom.

Interviewee
Sukit Prasithiran, Marketing Director

Share with us a little about the beginnings of your brand. What gave you the initial push? What was the gap and opportunity you saw in the market?

"We created Bath & Bloom while chatting among friends in a nice café. We graduated from the same university and met quite often after graduation. One of the things we thought of doing was starting a business together.

"We thought of having a coffee shop at first, but it required too heavy an investment for us at that time, so we opted to do something related to natural products.

"One of our partners has sensitive skin and can't use ordinary soap. The first product we created was a natural soap, and this became the seed for our brand. We wanted people of all types to take a soothing bath and be happy with bath time.

"Hence our name – when you take a bath, you bloom.

"We saw a big opportunity for our product, as at that time (in the early 2000s), there were not many natural skin-care products on the market, and Thailand offered lots of opportunities for choosing natural herbs and scents to be part of our products.

"We foresaw that people in future would care about their health more and try to use more natural products (or at least less chemicals) in their daily lives.

"With this opportunity and our forecast, we started the brand, eventually expanding our product line from natural soap to natural skincare, and further to home fragrances and now even hygiene products."

Did you recognise a trend or consumer insight that you could tap into?

"We saw a growing desire to use natural products in daily life, a wish to 'return to nature'. We ourselves believe that simple and natural products are the best for the people and for the environment.

"That's why we named our company Earth Factory Co., Ltd. We wanted to build a factory that cares for the Earth."

How do you differentiate your brand from the other players in your segment?

"Our brand is simple and quite straightforward. Customers can understand easily what we are offering to them. Our brand is friendly to everyone, regardless of sex or age, as well as to the environment.

"That said, although our brand might look simple, the details are sophisticated. If you look closer, we do have details on every part of the product.

En Toute Saison
All Year Round
BATH&BLOOM
Au Printemps
Avril
Diffuser Oil
BATH&BLOOM
Au Printemps
Mars
Diffuser Oil
BATH&BLOOM
Au Printemps
Mai
Diffuser Oil
En Toute Saison
All Year Round
BATH&BLOOM

THAI
JASMINE
SHAMPOO

“For example, our scents are lovingly formulated. Like Thai jasmine. Every brand has this scent, but we would say that our Thai jasmine is the best one – the ‘most jasmine’ scent – out there!

“This is how we differentiate ourselves from other brands – by producing goods as close to nature as possible.

“Packaging and design are also carefully considered. A product has to be beautiful but should also be convenient for usage. We care about how customers experience our products – eye-catching look, smooth touch, beautiful scent, convenient usage and good for decoration. Last but not least, it should be good for our environment as well.”

How would you define your target group? Do you differentiate your message to appeal to different needs?

“We believe our target group consists of people like us who are fond of using good-quality products with simple but elegant design. We are not too sensitive to price if that price reflects the quality and design.

“Our users are people who care about more than just the product’s function, but also the emotions or good experience the product contributes to their lifestyle. They don’t like to be outstanding among the crowd but rather be outstanding in their mind.”

When building your brand, what was the biggest hurdle you faced and how did you overcome it?

"At first, the challenge was how to educate our customers on the difference between commercial skincare and natural skincare, as the cost was so different at that time. Then, it was how to differentiate from other brands in the market.

"We made sure to communicate with our customers, to help them understand our business core, that they were not just getting good quality but also natural scents and an overall uplifting experience from our product.

"We have also invested a lot in our shops' appearance, to make us stand out from other traditional Thai brands. We work with good designers to create unique designs.

"These efforts have paid off. It's clear that all aspects of the customer experience are essential to let our brand bloom in our customers' hearts."

How do you keep track of changing consumer preferences and behaviour that could impact your brand?

"We keep records for all customers from all channels both online and offline in order to see their preferences. Of course, feedback from customers provides fruitful information to develop our brand.

BATH&BLOOM
ULTIMATE HEALING
HAND CREAM
Natural & Gentle Care Formulated with
active ingredients Fresh Bio Technology
℮ 50 ml/1.69 fl.oz.

"We also look at data from our competitors to get a better sense of the big picture. For example, we check on competitors' online platforms to see which of their products sell well, and which don't. We even look at customer reviews on competitors' platforms, to learn how we can improve our own offering."

How has Covid-19 impacted your business and how did you react? Has Covid opened up new opportunities for you?

"Covid affected our business quite a lot. Our product benefits from physical interaction – handling and smelling. So at the start of the pandemic, it was difficult for us to sell our products to new customers.

"What we did was to introduce online sales and use influencers to build more customers. It took some trial-and-error at first, before we found success with this new strategy. Importantly, we collaborated with credible influencers who had our target customers as fans.

"We are seeing customers move towards online purchases, rather than coming to our brick-and-mortar stores. We have now gathered all our online channels (Facebook, Instagram, Line) into one program. This allows us to communicate with all our customers more organically.

"We use Google Analytics to understand customers' online journeys, such as their clicks, pageviews, search terms, engagement with ads, talking about our brand, etc. Coupled with records of our members' purchase history and feedback, this gives us valuable insights into trends and customer preferences.

"We can then create the right products for our customers, as well as market the products more effectively.

"Covid created the opportunity for a new market segment: sanitiser products. Thus, we created our new product line, our hygiene collection. This has given us a new portfolio and expanded our customer base. We also see opportunity to further expand our product line to hygiene products for household use in future."

Can your brand stretch and extend into other segments?

"We are thinking to expand our business to consumer product lines or service segments like hospitality and tourism. For the consumer product line, it may be hygienic home care products like laundry or bathroom products.

"For the hospitality and tourism line, if possible, we might have our own farm to produce key raw materials for our products, and open it for visitors and tourists, to let them learn more about our brand first-hand."

Where do you see your brand in five to ten years' time, in terms of business offer, geography, target groups?

"We wish to see our brand become a global brand, with shops or online presence in most of the major cities in the world.

"We are looking to broaden our target group, to include mothers and children, as well as seniors. People of all generations need special products to take care of their skin and lifestyle.

"Finally, we hope to grow the business upstream and downstream, so that we can control quality every step of the way. Customers can then be doubly assured that they are receiving a product of the highest quality whenever they buy from us."

LESSONS FROM COVID

- **Digital is important but it isn't everything. Some brands need smell and touch. Keep some physical locations to create that experience.**

- **Use influencers and your brand's fans. They can be more credible and relatable when only online outreach is possible.**

- **Pivot to something that is urgently needed – in this case, sanitisers. Understand your target's needs and think about how you can extend the brand to fulfil them.**

SO YOU WANT TO START A BRAND? #2

Relevance

RELEVANCE IS the cornerstone of the whole brand you're building. If your idea, your product or service is not relevant to your target group, you can forget everything else. They simply won't care.

So, to begin, you ask yourself: Relevant – for whom? In order to answer that question, you need to have an idea of who your target group is. Because different promises are relevant to different people.

And don't say your target group is "everybody". First of all, it's probably not true, and secondly, you're making life difficult for yourself if you want to appeal to everybody. How will you choose design, communication channels, your tone of voice if you need to appeal to both the 57-year-old auntie in the suburbs and the 17-year-old teenager in the city? You need to choose.

Then, once you have chosen your target group, get to know them. How do they live, what are their needs, their dreams and worries? What do they want from life – and how can your brand, your service fulfil that need? If you have done your homework, identified a gap in the market that you can fill better than anybody else, because of who you are, then you're relevant to the target group.

E-mobility at Its Best

VINFAST

VIETNAM

VinFast is a car maker at the cutting edge. Within 21 months of launching in Vietnam, it became the #1 car seller in all its market segments. In 2022, it launches its smart EVs (electric vehicles) on the global stage, putting it squarely in the major league.

I still remember a meeting in early 2017 when I sat down with my colleagues in the Audi global HQ in Ingolstadt.

"How should we position our first fully electric car, the Audi E-tron?" someone asked. "As soon as we mention electric cars, people will think Tesla."

True, the US carmaker pretty much invented the segment and – with the help of its larger-than-life founder Elon Musk – has been dominating it ever since.

It took a visit to our advertising agency in San Francisco a few months later for us to hear the solution. The line they suggested was "Electric has gone Audi."

I loved it. Instead of "Audi has gone electric", which has a bit of a follower vibe, "Electric has gone Audi" was leveraging the over 100 years of Audi history, from Le Mans wins to quattro, engineering firsts to interior quality and design.

Since then, all mainstream car manufacturers have launched their own fully-electric models (whether because they truly believe in carbon-reduction or because stricter carbon dioxide caps make it a necessity), and new electric car brands like the successful PoleStar (from Geely via Volvo) have sprung up, offering a product that has overcome most of the initial challenges like build quality or limited range.

I have been interested in VinFast ever since I first read about them in a business paper – impressed that a relatively small market like Vietnam could produce a new global car manufacturer that offers cars precisely tailored to the target users' needs.

And VinFast means business. In March 2022, it was announced that they were building a US$2 billion factory in North Carolina to produce batteries, electric buses and SUVs.

The old rule still holds true: If you understand your target group and position your product as an answer to their needs, you have a good chance to succeed in the market, especially one that is far from saturated.

Interviewee
Đào Thị Thu Hiền, Global Communications Team (Vingroup)

About VinFast's beginnings, what gave you the initial push? And what was the market gap or opportunity you saw?

"VinFast was initially based on the needs of the Vietnamese market. Vietnam's automotive market has one of the highest potential in the world, thanks to an extremely low rate of car ownership of only 23 cars per 1,000 people (according to Seasia's report in October 2019).

"The domestic auto industry is limited to imports, insignificant localised assembly, underdeveloped supporting industries, and higher costs than other regional countries.

"In addition, the development of domestic automotive brands has been a goal of the Vietnamese government and its people for decades. These factors drove the beginning of VinFast, before the brand looked towards global trends.

"From a global perspective, the electric vehicle (EV) revolution is ripe for opportunity and acceleration. Many of the world's developed countries are pursuing a path towards EVs, and consumers are open and ready for this new era. Meanwhile, the EV industry is still in its early stages of development. Although competition is growing, there is still room for newcomers to break through.

"VinFast is hence entering the global market with the potential of more than 1 billion gasoline-powered cars to be replaced by EVs, as well as a wave of inspired young consumers who are eager to have EVs as their first vehicle.

"While automotive companies are new to the competition for global market share, these initial stages of the EV movement represent VinFast' best opportunity to emerge as a key player among the world's leading EV brands.

"The last four years have shown that VinFast is on the right track. VinFast vehicles continuously rank first in their respective segments in the Vietnamese market, In particular, VinFast's first EV model achieved a sales record of 25,000 pre-orders in only three months. VinFast has become the most popular car company in Vietnam.

"In the global market, VinFast has made a splash at international product exhibitions and has received tremendous feedback. VinFast is approaching its goal of becoming a global smart EV brand."

Which market trends or information did VinFast use when setting its vision?

"Electrification is an irreversible trend globally. Many of the world's developed countries are pursuing a path towards electric vehicles with beneficial policies for EV companies and limiting or even halting the production of gasoline-powered vehicles to protect the environment.

ABB

“Technology is developing tremendously fast and becoming increasingly intelligent. Unlike traditional gasoline-powered vehicles, EVs still have plenty of room to apply new technologies. Electric vehicles are not just simple transportation – they are a smart space where users can experience multiple conveniences while they drive.

“Additionally, consumer perception is increasingly changing in favour of switching to green, smart, environmentally friendly transportation.

“This is the foundation for the automotive revolution in the market as well as the ground for us to realise that EVs are the future of mobility and to set out our vision: driving the movement of the global smart electric vehicle revolution.”

How do you differentiate your brand from the other players in your segment?

“High-quality products, reasonable prices, and outstanding service are the three core components that enable VinFast to win customers in Vietnam. These are the drivers that will dictate VinFast’s competitive strategy in international markets.

“VinFast models have a modern and luxurious design, and meet the high-quality standards of American and European markets, with a 4-5 stars NCAP safety rating.

"In terms of affordability, VinFast applies flexible financial solutions to ensure that our cars are easily accessible to more potential car buyers. With EV products, VinFast's battery rental business model provides a breakthrough solution that significantly reduces the cost of car ownership and allows its cars to compete with gasoline-powered vehicles.

"As for after-sales service, we have an outstanding warranty policy that extends up to ten years, allowing customers to feel confident with their electric vehicles for a considerable time. VinFast also has market-leading standards for quality after-sales service such as customer care and repair.

"We are confident that VinFast will be welcomed in our target markets because of our quality EV models, flexible and innovative sales policies, and our dedicated Asian-style after-sales service."

How would you define your target group? Do you have any special strategies to attract those target groups with different needs?

"VinFast's strategy is to provide high-standard products, reasonable prices, and outstanding service to compete directly with gasoline-powered cars. Thus, we target customers who want to experience powerful vehicles with spacious cabins that are smart, safe and environmentally friendly."

VF e35

When building your brand, what was the biggest hurdle you faced and how did you overcome it?

"Our first hurdle is that EVs have not reached widespread acceptance yet. Thus, we have to educate consumers so they can easily switch from internal combustion engine (ICE) cars to EVs with peace of mind.

"Secondly, EVs have a high price due to the high cost of vehicle components such as batteries. EVs also have a limited range and are subject to battery quality risks.

"VinFast has developed strategies to overcome these challenges. In terms of batteries, we have commenced the construction of the large-scale VinES battery factory to ensure self-sufficient supply while providing a variety of suitable batteries for VinFast's electric vehicles. We also cooperate with the world's leading reputable battery suppliers and start-up companies to research and apply the most advanced battery technologies, such as super-fast charging, 100% solid-state batteries, and more.

"In terms of the pricing barrier and battery depreciation, we apply a battery rental policy with the same cost as a gasoline-powered car, with a warranty of up to ten years, bringing peace of mind to customers."

One way to create something new is to disrupt convention. What are you disrupting and how?

"Speed, one of the core values of VinFast and Vingroup, is a key factor facilitating our disruption of the automotive industry.

"In terms of production, VinFast does not follow a certain archetype on how to design and develop products for customers. To accelerate production, we focus on internal R&D, while also connecting globally to deliver world-class quality products with advanced technologies.

"In addition to cooperating with world-leading partners such as Pininfarina, Cerence, Gotion Hi-tech, and others, Vingroup has built a technology ecosystem specialising in researching and applying AI platforms, big data, and machine learning to develop advanced technologies for our car models.

"In terms of products, the product strategy is tailored to consumer needs and operating conditions of specific markets. In terms of service, as mentioned, our after-sales service surpasses existing market norms."

How does VinFast track changes in consumer preferences and behaviour that may affect the brand?

"VinFast and all the companies within Vingroup have a unique approach to their customers. In Vietnam, we proudly affirm that our products and services can serve most of our customers' needs. Therefore, we study consumer behaviours across multiple categories and touch-points. In addition, we also actively connect with global experts and market leaders to thoroughly understand the needs of customers in each market we operate in."

How has Covid impacted your business and how did you react? Has Covid opened up new opportunities for you?

"Covid-19 has affected millions of businesses worldwide and VinFast is no exception. However, the positive thing is that we made good use of this difficult time to reorganise our operating system, management strategy, human resources, and working methods to run more effectively.

"Thanks to that, VinFast is still one of Vietnam's top car companies with the best sales records in recent times.

"We have also upgraded other fundamental systems during the pandemic. We are promoting the development of domestic industries, restructuring the supply chain to

VINFAST

reduce our dependence on external sources, and diversifying our sales methods.

"We are also developing our digital sales (e-commerce) platform, virtual reality (VR) applications, livestream sales (live broadcasts), and telesales (video-calling services). Furthermore, we are applying automation in production, using robots and smart technologies to replace and support humans.

"An example of the success of these strategies can be seen in the pre-orders for our VF e34. Out of the 25,000 pre-orders, an astounding 10,000 orders were made online."

Where do you see your brand in five to ten years' time?

"Our vision is 'Driving the movement of the global smart electric vehicle revolution'. We believe we are well on track!"

LESSONS FROM COVID

- **Use downtime to reorganise your system – from HR to operations, production to management to supply chain.**

- **Reduce dependence on others. What can you bring in-house?**

- **Use digital tools like Virtual Reality and live-streaming to connect with your target market.**

SO YOU WANT TO START A BRAND? #3

Differentiation

YOU MAY BE RELEVANT – but you may not be the only one. Other brands – those that are similar to yours or very different – may fill the same gap, fulfil the same need. Their promise may also be relevant to the target group.

Just being something consumers would consider isn't enough. Why? Because when faced with two offerings that are exactly the same, smart consumers will always choose the cheaper one. And why shouldn't they?

So if you're relevant but not differentiated from the competition, you may need to compete on price. Which is a war that is very hard to win. Because the only way to compete on price is to be cheaper than the competition. Undercut them. Then they undercut you, then you undercut them. And so on. Not a situation you want to be in.

Instead, think about how you can be different. Consumers are prepared to pay a little extra – if you can give them a good reason for it. Maybe you're adding something to the product, like an extra benefit. But be careful – those are easy for the competition to copy. Remember the one camera lens, two camera lenses, three camera lenses competition between mobile phone brands? Easy to copy, hard to own.

Maybe it's a service that comes with the product. Or some personalisation. Or a personal touch that comes with that service. These don't necessarily have to cost more. Just a bit of thinking, a bit of training, a bit of rewarding for your staff. These are much harder to steal or copy. Because they are rooted in culture – which is hard to build and takes time to create.

Design can be a good differentiator because it is emotional. The way you communicate your brand with photography and clever copy can also position it up – give it a more premium perception – so that consumers who want to express that about themselves can use your brand for it.

So think about how you can be different – in a relevant way.

Bridging the Gap Between College and Career

KINOBI

SINGAPORE

Kinobi is a standout in Asia's vibrant edtech scene. Partnering with an extensive network of universities, the platform is helping the burgeoning ranks of smart young Southeast Asians make the leap from school to the professional world – all in a playful, digital way.

Benjamin Wong is a former student, and for a while I'd observed his career path – from beginnings in private equity and a family office to the search for a more meaningful challenge, something that gives back.

Kinobi

I remember an evening at Kinobi's first office – one small room behind a barber shop in Singapore's Geylang red light district – during the first weeks of the pandemic. The room was filled to the brink with young, enthusiastic students looking after marketing, recruiting and sponsoring. Very little furniture, but a good bottle of whisky that was shared in small measures between all.

The gap in the market that Kinobi addresses has been apparent for a while: bridging between college and career, helping people with their positioning, their CV, their skills and interview behaviour. And all of that in way that understands and appeals to the target group, from Singapore to Indonesia, Vietnam to Malaysia.

What most impresses me most is the drive, motivation and attitude of all the people working with Kinobi. Ben has already understood what most HR practitioners take years to realise: Skills can be taught, but attitude is something you should look for in your hires from the very start.

Interviewee
Benjamin Wong, Founder and CEO

Share with us about the beginnings of your brand. What gave you the initial push? What was the gap and opportunity you saw in the market?

"I was an avid player of MapleStory when I was younger, playing through my Primary School Leaving Examinations. There were guides online teaching me how to get from Level 1 to 200 as a Magician, the different classes I could choose from, where and which monsters I should fight from Level 20 to 30 to level up, and even which weapons and armour I should purchase for which stats!

"But, for something more serious as our careers and jobs, there was a lack of guidance. It is strange that we treat our games with more intense focus!

"Thus, I built Kinobi to solve that last-mile gap between college and careers, as students get into the 'adulting' phase. The name Kinobi is a nod to Obi-wan Kenobi's guidance to Anakin Skywalker."

Did you recognise a trend or consumer insight that you could tap into?

"It's really a golden age for Southeast Asia, especially for the developing countries, which are brimming with potential to grow. In a country like Indonesia, for example, there's a lot of support from family offices, government and organisations in bringing up the skills of their youths.

"Our goal from the start was to support and build youths seeking to grow in their career and reach their dream jobs. We believed that the way to reach them was through the various career centres situated in every university.

"Most career centres are overstretched, with two staff handling thousands of students. They are burdened with a lot of administrative tasks, such as having to 'index-match' student names and serial numbers to have a complete picture of what their student outcomes are. Many are frustrated because they have a passion for speaking to students, not speaking to data. We saw a huge opportunity here to penetrate the market.

"At the same time, most Tier 2 universities do not have the necessary resources, and thus outsource their career centre to us. Partnering with them was a natural outreach for the many students under their umbrella and allowed us to reach a much wider audience.

"Finally, we are Asian. Imagine the anathema if you told your parents you did not want to finish your schooling with a university degree!"

How do you differentiate your brand from other players in your segment?

"Comprehensiveness and relatability. Every single tool needed for job prepping is available on one platform, from resumes to interviews to researching. Everything you need to achieve your dream job can be found in one place.

“This also makes sense for the career centres, because a big pain point that they face is having to gel the data together to have a unified picture of their students. No more VLOOKUPs or pivot tables to present to the board.

“As for relatability, it means we keep up with developments and trends, so as to provide our target demographic with the latest offerings, and make life as simple for them as possible.

“For example, we constantly adapt to the media channels used most often by youths, e.g. TikTok, Instagram. We are the leaders in the education segment within TikTok, and lead the way in several countries.

“Our resume builder uses Artificial Intelligence (AI) to make creating a resume a simple process. Writing a resume usually seems like a daunting task. Thus we show step-by-step what you should do, what content you can focus on, and how you should write, using suggested phrases from our AI.”

How would you define your target group? Do you differentiate your message to appeal to different needs?

“Our end user is really the student. Career success is more important for Gen Zs than any generation. More debt, less

STUDENTS
UNIVERSITY
EMPLOYER
Kinobi
EN
LOGIN
SIGN UPFOR FREE
All-In-One Platform to Prepare Your Career
Get hired within weeks by building perfect resumes, practicing for interviews, and learning from our courses.
START PREPARING
KINOBI FOR UNIVERSITY ›

CREATE RESUME
Katy Kat
WORK EXPERIENCE
Company Name · Singapore
Jan 2020 - Present
• First point of experience
• Second point of experience
ASK QUESTIONS
Katy
BUSINESS STUDENT
Hi coach! I have some questions about my resume and career I'd like your help with
May 2020 - Jan 2020
Hafiz
HEAD COACH AT KINOBI
Hey Kat! Great to have you at Kinobits. Ask away! I'm here to help.
Jul 2017 - Jun 2020
Jul 2014 - Jun 2017
••• AND MANY MORE!
450,000+
Current active user
10,000+
Resumes created weekly
120+
Hours of courses content
60+
University partners

earnings and higher unemployment. In this case, we rolled out scholarships, which is more effective in increasing awareness than buying ads on Google or Instagram.

"Our unique value proposition for them is that we empower them. Unlike on other platforms where they feel inadequate when they apply for a top job, with our platform, they feel empowered. They feel, 'Yes! I can achieve this job, because I have the tools within reach to upskill myself and practise my interviews to get it.'

"However, it is the career centre that foots the bill. For them, students are their priority. We help them to easily track student outcomes. We create a knowledge centre and a career centre network where they can learn best practices from our white papers, as well as networking sessions with career centre heads around the world."

When building your brand, what was the biggest hurdle you faced and how did you overcome it?

"The biggest mistake is to assume what your customer needs, without truly listening to them.

"In the beginning, we thought the students wanted to 'get fit' in a career sense. Thus, they would stick to a routine and would be willing to adopt the best habits (e.g. eat 'salad') in order to achieve that goal. However, they all didn't like salad. It was too tough to commit to, and what they wanted was to feel good about their own efforts.

They wanted to eat 'Indomie'. Thus, we started creating content that was more 'fast-food' focused, and that boomed.

"We increased our month-on-month growth to almost 1.5x each month because we hit the pain point of students. Most are lost and want the solution right away.

"Brand is not what you create. It is how others perceive you."

One way to create something new is to disrupt convention. What are you disrupting and how?

"We are revolutionising the system of career education by providing a centralised platform that can connect all stakeholders. Rather than leaving university career centres to struggle aimlessly with limited resources, we become their back-office and data management system, providing everything they want, already developed and built specifically for them.

"Under our Kinobi programme, career centre counsellors and staff are able to access the admin dashboard where they can view and analyse all their students at one go while granting them the connections and network with companies offering internship programmes or entry-level jobs. It's half the work but twice the results for the career centre."

Kinobi
Kinobi
Kinobi

Kinobi
Kinobi
Kinobi

How do you keep track of changing consumer preference and behaviour that could impact your brand?

"Not much has changed drastically since we started, but if we had to identify one thing, it would be the volatile nature of social media trends.

"As mentioned earlier, in order to be more relatable to the youths, we have adapted to the common channels used by these youths, such as TikTok and Instagram.

"Especially on a platform like TikTok, where garnering a strong following depends on keeping up with the latest trends, there has to be an intentional effort in relating to youths. This also applies to our other work on Instagram and even our weekly newsletter, which we added memes to.

"One thing we've done that has helped this endeavour tremendously is to hire our Social Media Associates from among this generation. With the help of these individuals, it has become much easier to ensure our content is appropriate to our target audience and not just depend on our own biased understanding of what's interesting.

"Finally, being a watch collector and an NFT project co-founder, I am aware of how quickly trends change. We take best practices from how the best brands and media outlets market brands – from VICE to Hodinkee, and how Hermes does white-glove services, for example – and incorporate many FMCG (fast-moving consumer goods) ideas into edtech."

How has Covid impacted your business and how did you react? Has Covid opened up new opportunities for you?

"Our presence has become even more pivotal because of Covid. Research by Stamford has shown that recessions cause graduates to be set back in terms of financial growth by 10–15 years. This is a big difference compared to their counterparts finding their success in much less turbulent waters.

"Thus, especially now, the need for quality career guidance is even more essential in providing graduates with the tools they need to succeed."

Can your brand stretch and extend into other segments?

"There are several things that the Kinobi brand can do. We are essentially the platform where we hold all the data about people's careers. It would be very cool to predict who goes to what jobs even before starting.

"Imagine Grab being able to pinpoint who is going to be a good fit for their digital marketing department when the individual is only in their first year of university. That is immensely powerful.

"This unified algorithm of employment and skills could also be used by governments to improve the standard of living for people all across the world.

"Our platform is not just a 'first job' for many. It is the first of many other things: a first insurance, a first bank account, a first car, a first housing loan, a first investment plan, a first crypto wallet."

Where do you see your brand in five to ten years' time, in terms of business offer, geography, target groups?

"'Kinobi helped me find my first job' – I want this to be the byword of every single 18–25-year-old across the world. To do that, we have to be the essential application and tool among universities and governments across Southeast Asia and globally, and embedded into the undergraduate system in a way that students and career centres can't do without it."

LESSONS FROM COVID

- **Look at how Covid has impacted peoples' lives, and position yourself to help them bridge the "Covid gap".**

- **Build online platforms for learning; make it fun.**

- **Use digital channels to connect with your users, and adapt to the style of each platform, e.g. TikTok vs Instagram.**

SO YOU WANT TO START A BRAND? #4

Consistency

AFTER YOU HAVE found a positioning that is both relevant to your target group and differentiated from the competition, think about how this positioning of your new brand is going to be expressed through touchpoints – every point where the consumer meets the brand.

The messaging expressed by each of these touchpoints needs to be consistent.

So make a long list of every single point where someone would get in touch with your brand. Start with those you control, like naming, logo, colours, packaging, website, copy, images, brick-and-mortar stores, the founder's image, customer service, your people, etc. Then move on to those that are much harder for you to control but would often be seen as belonging to your brand – like any online marketplaces you're on, delivery services, your customers (they write reviews), etc.

The point is to avoid sending mixed messages. When your positioning is "The Listening Brand" but it takes 90 minutes to speak to customer service on the phone, that's a disconnect, a mixed message.

As consumers, we all believe our own experiences more than any advertising messages we receive from brands, so all your investment in media and creative would have been wasted in this case.

A Healthier Marketplace

KURLY

KOREA

Imagine ordering your groceries before you go to sleep and having it on your doorstep at dawn – fresh as fresh can be. Kurly spotted this gap in 2015, and became a huge success in Seoul. Then when the Covid-19 lockdowns hit, the brand simply shot through the roof.

When I lived in Seoul between 2013 and 2016, my shopping world was pretty much still a brick-and-mortar experience.

I'd walk over to COEX and the connected Hyundai department store for anything special; for the day-to-day groceries there was a Lotte My Super at the back of my house where I picked up fruit and vegetables. Not a great experience, but it was convenient.

Then Covid hit, and convenience turned into necessity. All over the world, delivery apps started offering to bring to your home hot cooked food or just a box of groceries. Even after strict movement restrictions were lifted, the demand for this convenience remained. This demand will stay strong, enabled by a substantial number of people continuing to work from home.

So how do you stand out in this busy field? How do you give customers a reason to choose your brand that goes beyond price and product?

Kurly has found a brilliant answer by combining time and product. Instead of offering conserved or frozen food, their promise is "fresh", supported by the logistical miracle of delivering the order by 7 a.m. the next morning.

So even for customers who go back to the office, Kurly provides a healthy and quick alternative to going to the supermarket.

I wish I was back in Korea.

Interviewees
Kyung Ah, Nam; and Jae Yeon, Yoon, Brand Marketing Specialists

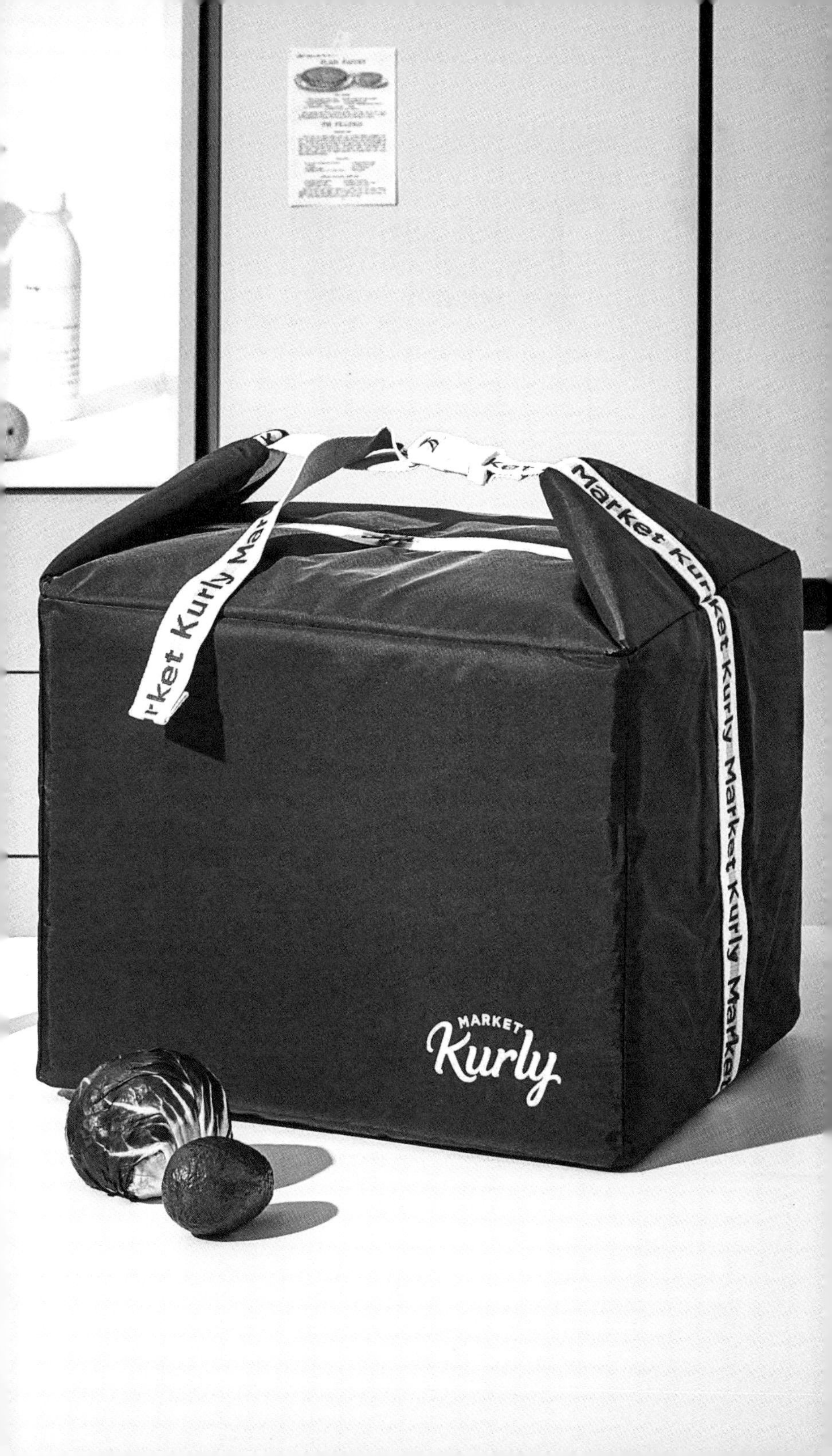
MARKET
Kurly

Share with us about the beginnings of your brand. What was the gap and opportunity you saw in the market?

"In 2015, Kurly's team members had the idea of making life better for people, and they were looking for areas yet untapped.

"At that time, consumers in Korea always had to check if there was a shopping mart near their house. Even if there was, it was still difficult to be sure whether the products sold at the mart were of good quality. At the same time, marts were getting bigger, and offering more and more choices for consumers to choose from.

"As a result, shopping often felt stressful.

"Ordering groceries online had its own problems. First, people found it hard to trust the product even though they had paid money to use the delivery service. In addition, no company that dealt in distribution gave much information on how good products were discovered or explained them well to consumers.

"These were the problems that our team members had as consumers. The members who were conscious of this problem and who believed that delicious food is the greatest joy came together as a team.

"For myself, as a picky housewife who wants to find the best products, I have always thought that innovation is needed in the distribution industry. I asked myself: 'If I treat food the way I work in the high-tech industry, maybe I can feel the joy of changing the quality of my life.'"

Did you recognise a trend or consumer insight that you could tap into?

"We wanted to create a service for those who find it difficult to shop in various places and are more careful and demanding when choosing ingredients. It is because they believe that a person's life can change a lot depending on what and how they eat.

"We decided to select as well as grow produce for these customers. We went all over the country, looking for the healthiest produce, and tried them one by one, choosing agricultural products that were raised with honesty. We then thought of ways for our customers to eat healthy produce as fresh as possible.

"The key factor, we found, is Time.

"In today's busy society, grocery delivery at dawn would bring consumers the most value. Customers could order before they went to sleep, and their delivery would greet them in the morning the next day.

"And from the producers' point of view, there is nothing more upsetting than having good produce being damaged or going bad during the delivery process. Early-morning

MARKET
Kurly
HALLO!
MARKET
Kurly
ALL
PAPER
CHALLENGE

MARKET
Kurly

TARTUFI
Morra
WHITE TRUFFLE
DROPS
Ingredients
Olive oil, Flavours
Net Weight: 250 ml
LEONARDI
1871
Condimento
Balsamico
Bianco
10
White Balsamic
Condiment
ITALY

delivery was thus the one and only way to satisfy both consumers and producers."

How do you differentiate your brand from the other players in your segment?

"Up until now, the key variable for retailers to strike a balance between consumers and suppliers has been the price. Retailers try to offer a reasonable price to the customer and to guarantee a set fair price to the supplier.

"The way in which Kurly balances these two sides is different. From the beginning, Kurly focused on the product, not the price. A distribution system is meaningful only when good products are used as a medium. Without good products, you cannot be a good platform.

"Kurly thus asks the producers for the price they are willing to accept, instead of determining the supply price based on the distributor's margin. Thereafter, the product is priced by taking into account distribution and incidental costs, before it is offered to consumers.

"The reason we choose to sell 100% of our products directly to consumers is because we want the producers to be able to focus on the quality without the burden of having to keep stock, which is often expensive.

"Under the motto of 'providing good products at reasonable prices', Kurly creates a positive-sum game that benefits all three players: the customer can get a valuable product; the supplier can get a reasonable delivery price; and the platform can make a reasonable profit.

"In our quest to bring in good products, Kurly pursues four avenues: first, securing good suppliers by visiting local producers and famous suppliers across the country; second, by adding existing well-known suppliers; third, by improving products together with the suppliers; and fourth, by creating Kurly's own unique products.

"In addition, Kurly has developed a curation service with the aim of providing differentiated experiences in the distribution industry. Our product selection criteria is also constantly being refined, based on market potential, design, content consistency, taste, and consistency with the company's philosophy and strategy. We have also established processes for listening and responding to customer feedback.

"As a result, the 'direction desired by the customer' has become the common goal shared by Kurly and its suppliers. This is how Kurly's differentiated product competitiveness is achieved in the fiercely competitive industry."

How would you define your target group? Do you differentiate your message to appeal to different needs?

"Kurly's core target is people who have a strong preference for good quality – families who value the quality of

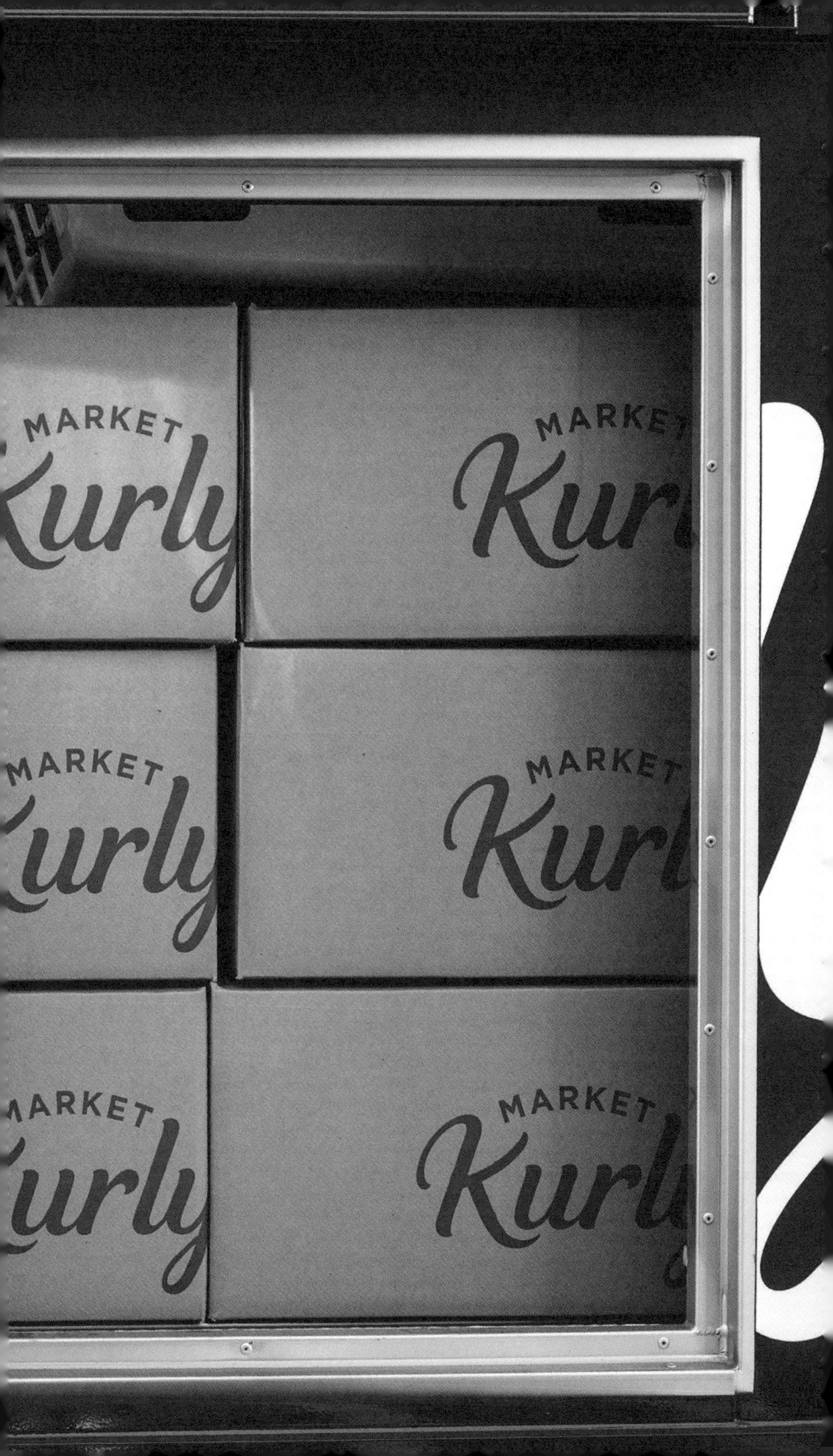

MARKET
Kurly

www.kurly.com

MARKET
Kurly
www.kurly.com
MARKET
Kurly

ingredients for healthy meals, dual-income couples who want to receive reliable products with comfort, single or two-member households who value consumption for themselves.

"In order to attract new customers, Kurly runs promotions such as our '100 Won Deals'. We are also conducting a new trial promotion that allows new customers to experience an 'A-ha!' moment when receiving their boxes the very next morning after placing their first order – and then be 'locked in' to Kurly.

"Kurly Lovers is our tiered membership system, where consumers are awarded benefits for each level they reach, from General (less than 150,000 won paid in the previous month), to Friends (more than 150,000 won paid in the previous month), to Purple (more than 1 million won paid).

"We actively recommend products to our customers, based on their consumption patterns. As the number of products increases, we want our customers to come into contact with good products they may not be aware of."

When building your brand, what was the biggest hurdle you faced? How did you overcome it?

"The biggest concern was to be sure of how many consumers would recognise the quality we were offering. One question that hung over us was: There had been many distributors before – why weren't they successful?

"First, we had to prove that there was a clear demand, and we had to show that we could fulfil it with our unique way of sourcing and selection. We put a lot of effort into making one or two successful cases.

"For example, we put a lot of effort into the products of the early suppliers at the start of Kurly. To convince customers that a product was good, we called all those who had bought it. We checked if they understood what was written on the product detail page. We explained how to store, prepare and consume the product to get the best out of it. We believed that consumers who understood these things would appreciate the true value of the products, and would thus come back again.

"In addition, stabilising early morning deliveries was also a challenge, particularly in the case of minimising wastage of fresh food. Every day, we would forecast the daily supply and the customers' orders. If the forecast was incorrect, we were not able to deliver the product to some of the customers.

"In order to minimise these errors, we have invested heavily in building a data analysis system. It is able to predict demand and make decisions using algorithms and machine learning, drawing on the data from all our channels.

"As a result, we maintain a product discard rate of less than 1%, which is lower than the general 2–3% discard rate of other marts."

One way to create something new is to disrupt convention. What are you disrupting and how?

“Kurly’s early morning delivery service completely disrupted the existing distribution paradigm in Korea and opened a new era of delivery.

“Before, it was normal to order goods on the Internet and wait four or five days to receive them. However, with the entry of giant e-commerce competitors into the market, the delivery duration was greatly reduced to one or two days, as distributors performed delivery without going through a delivery company.

“Against this background, Kurly rolled out our dawn delivery service. Dawn delivery allows orders to be placed as late as midnight, with deliveries guaranteed to arrive by 7 a.m. the next day.

“Kurly’s logistics subsidiary Fresh Solution supports this by reducing the time taken to get produce to consumers’ homes. Using refrigerated trucks, Kurly operates a ‘full cold chain’ system that maintains the optimal storage temperature for each product from the point of production to the point of delivery.

“In addition, Kurly is continuing to innovate in the area of packaging materials. Under our All Paper Challenge, we aim to phase out plastic packaging and to find sustainable alternatives that care for the environment.

"For example, we have launched the Purple Box, a reusable packaging made of waterproof nylon on the surface and cellular polystyrene for thermal insulation.

"These cases of Kurly's disruptive innovation have not only changed the delivery market, but also changed consumers' everyday life."

How do you keep track of changing consumer preference and behaviour that could impact your brand?

"The only way to keep track of rapidly changing consumer trends is by listening to our customers and being a consumer-centric brand.

"Our Customer Initiative (CI) team offers our customers benefits that are optimised for individual consumption patterns. For example, customers are categorised by the membership system according to the amount they spend every month. Each target group receives daily customised push messages from the CI team.

"In addition, by implementing marketing activities such as rewards or coupons, the CI team accelerates new user acquisition and strengthens user retention.

"Meanwhile, in order to minimise customer complaints, our Customer Communications (CC) team plays an important role in listening to customers' highly detailed expectations and wishes – the 'Voice of the

MARKET
Kurly

MARKET
Kurly
Market Kurly
Market Kurly
MARKET
Kurly

Customer' (VOC). These days, customers have extremely high standards and expectations.

"As a result, Kurly places daily VOCs at the top of the corporate agenda and shares the related issues in real time. If a VOC with important keywords such as 'child', 'birthday', 'damage' or 'hurt' is found in a product review, the CC team flags the issue as urgent and responds immediately.

"We believe that flexibly managing unexpected customer complaints is as important as identifying customers' potential needs. That's why Kurly strives to respond to VOCs promptly, systematically and thoroughly.

"Finally, the Brand Marketing team monitors social media platforms such as Instagram, blogs and online communities to hear the customer's voice from outside. There are more than 500,000 posts about Kurly on Instagram and Naver, South Korea's largest internet portal site. We derive consumer insights by discovering what customers want, how they felt about Kurly, what was good and what was disappointing."

How has Covid-19 impacted your business and how did you react? Has Covid opened up new opportunities?

"Ever since the pandemic, e-commerce orders have skyrocketed, and sales on e-commerce channels increased by 34%. Food sales surged 92% from the previous year.

"In addition, as people in their 50s and 60s who did not use e-commerce became more familiar with mobile shopping, they began to actively join the services previously used only by the younger generations.

"During the pandemic, order volume exceeded the range we could offer every day, and this continues even now in this Covid-endemic era. Consumers have had their eyes opened to the convenience that Kurly brings, and they will be more likely to stay on the channel even after the coronavirus crisis is over."

Can your brand stretch and extend into other segments?

"Kurly initially focused on the fresh food category but has gradually expanded into a comprehensive mall that includes many non-food categories. The fact that Kurly thoroughly inspects all products and delivers them safely and quickly bolsters the positive response from customers.

"We are expanding into the non-food sector because our customers want to purchase non-food items together with food items while shopping online. Beauty, pet food, home appliances, flowers, and hotel accommodation vouchers are on the rise, and recently, airline tickets and rental car reservation services have been added.

"In the future, we will continue to strive to provide the assortment of products that customers want from Kurly."

Where do you see your brand in five to ten years' time, in terms of business offer, geography, target groups?

"Recently, Kurly is preparing for the domestic listing to go public. When it enters the Korea Exchange in 2022, it will become the No.1 K-Unicorn company that succeeded in listing. In preparation for the IPO, Kurly is making a number of moves to raise corporate value.

"First, Kurly is about to open its platform for individual sellers to sell their products along with items exclusively offered by the retailer.

"Second, Kurly is expanding its morning delivery service, which was only available in Seoul and the metro area, to Busan, Ulsan, Daejeon and Daegu.

"Finally, in terms of brand communication, as more customers now recognise Kurly as a top mobile grocery shopping brand, we are finding more ways to show the unique value that only Kurly can give. As more companies offer similar services to ours, we need to once in a while remind our customers why we were special in the first place.

"We are proud of our existing customers who have known us since the beginning, and of having become a brand that is loved in their daily lives."

LESSONS FROM COVID

- **Build up your e-commerce in a way that older customers can also access and use it – convenience is key.**

- **Understand new needs like health and freshness – and let them inform your brand positioning.**

- **Understand that delivery is here to stay – what is needed that you can deliver?**

SO YOU WANT TO START A BRAND? #5

What's in a Name?

ONCE YOU HAVE an idea for a startup, there are a million things to do: think about sourcing and production, get financing, find the best people, etc. That's why many founders don't spend enough time thinking about the brand at the beginning.

You cannot *not* have a brand. Your offer, product or service, as soon as it's out there in front of consumers, will be perceived as a brand. So either you think about who you want to be as a brand and how you want to be perceived – or they will do it for you.

One area where this oversight becomes very clear is naming. Your name (more than your logo, colours, fonts – even though they all play a part in brand perception) is the most important and the most immediate way to express what you stand for, what you're all about. We all know this. The first question we ask someone sitting next to us at uni or being introduced to us at a networking event is, "What's your name?"

The best name says what you need to know about the brand. Singapore Airlines? Ah, I see, an airline that comes from Singapore. Volkswagen? Great, a car for the people. This is by far the best way to name your new brand, because it makes the name work as hard as it can. Even if your brand's name is all people manage to catch, they have an idea.

A second way to name your brand isn't as hardworking, but at least it is not damaging. Make up a word or choose one that has no meaning whatsoever. There was a time when Google or Uniqlo didn't mean anything. If that's your preference, you've given yourself a task: you need to fill the word with meaning. It's not enough if people only catch the word – they need to learn what it stands for. And that takes money. Advertising money. And time. Time that you may not have.

The third way to name your brand – and the worst way – is to choose a word that already has a meaning, but it's not what you do. Brands tend to go for this solution because they think a certain word sounds cool, or they think that naming their (Asian) brand after a neighbourhood in Copenhagen will give it "European flair". Don't.

If you do this, you'll have to spend money and time not just to build awareness of your brand and its name, but also to make people change their mind about what the name means. People don't like to change their mind, so be prepared to spend more money and more time than you envisioned.

Peranakan Cakes and More

FIRST LOVE

INDONESIA

Must premium cakes be baked in-house? Indonesia's First Love Patisserie is disrupting this long-held assumption with its all-natural, preservative-free Mille Crepe cakes – centrally produced to exacting standards, and delivered fresh to mall stores across the region.

More than ten years ago, for a branding series I was hosting for Singapore's Channel NewsAsia, we went to Indonesia to look at some local brands. One of them was a bakery chain that produced fresh cakes in the back of the shop, and it was the first time that I discovered Indonesians' sweet tooth.

During the interview, I asked the brand owner about the balance between freshness (people prefer not to have preservatives in their pastries) and consistency (if produced locally, quality and taste may vary). Now it seems that one brand has managed to resolve this tension, by producing centrally and then delivering the fresh cakes to the outlets.

Despite the massive size of the Indonesian market, First Love Patisserie has set its eyes on an even bigger piece of the cake: China. By setting up cafes in China, the brand is creating scale while retaining some amount of foreignness, which often helps in China to appeal to customers and command a price premium.

An extra bonus: If there is a lockdown in one place where you operate, you can pivot and concentrate on a territory where sales are still possible.

Interviewee
Jonathan Ng, General Manager

first love
ミルクレープ

Share with us about the beginnings of your brand. What was the gap and opportunity you saw in the market?

“Back in 2009, when we first landed in Jakarta, the food business wasn’t in our business plan. But as we visited the malls, we were thrilled by the vibrancy. It was energetic, packed with people shopping, eating, hanging out.

“That’s when we saw we could introduce a unique never-done-before product into the market. And the best part is that it promotes better health and simplicity through quality ingredients and processes. Hence we created a simple brand: First Love.”

Did you recognise a trend or consumer insight that you could tap into?

“At that time, you could only find premium-priced cakes in hotels. Those offered in regular retail outlets were products with a lower price and lower quality. We immediately saw an opportunity to market this exclusive product, not only with premium quality, but also a pricing that could appeal to the masses.

“Today, we are considered to be the pioneer in premium cakes offered inside malls in Jakarta. By looking at the level of acceptance towards our brand, we know we have altered consumer perceptions. Consumers now go for better quality and healthier products over the price factor.

"Online social media helps us to create a more targeted marketing program for awareness, connection and retention. Having said that, we still continue to market with conventional method such as flyers, radio ads and food tasting events."

How do you differentiate your brand from the other players in your segment?

"Our company adopts a spirited culture toward building the tone of the brand. We look at the brand as a living person, someone we respect and love.

"From the making of the product to the packaging of it, our customers understand how much care goes into the whole process. We provide this detailed information at every touchpoint.

"Our continuous improvement in various aspects over time has kept us relevant, so that we are able to retain and grow our customer base."

How would you define your target group? Do you differentiate your message to appeal to different needs?

"The general perception of our brand is exclusive, premium and expensive. In reality, the majority of our customers are still the common consumer.

ミルクレープ

ERIE

"This has been a great positioning for us, as we are able to gain trust and acceptance from various segments of consumers. After all, they want to bring the best product home to celebrate memorable occasions with their loved ones.

"We do intentionally use a youthful tone in our online services to cater to the young and energetic market. We also hold special promotions for value-hunters online."

When building your brand, what was the biggest hurdle you faced and how did you overcome it?

"The biggest hurdle was marketing this product at a premium price. Our product was priced 30% higher than the competition when we first started. We were tempted to reduce the price numerous times.

"But we stayed consistent in our strategy, by focusing more on continued efforts in communicating our brand and its value for almost two years. We ultimately established our position in the market by the sheer power of word-of-mouth."

One way to create something new is to disrupt convention. What are you disrupting and how?

"In a typical bakery or patisserie setting, the products are made on the spot and sold. The perception is that the products are fresher this way. However, this method doesn't take into account many other aspects which are critical to the successful management of an outlet.

"For example, if the baker is not having a good day, the products could turn out with a different taste that day. If the baker is careless, the product could be done incorrectly. Even if the product is done well, sales for the day could be affected by weather or other unexpected situations. Sometimes production could be insufficient but there isn't enough time to produce more.

"To avoid these outcomes, outlets end up having to hire more people or better bakers. All this means that the outlet will have higher operating costs.

"What we have done is to take out as much uncertainty from the retail end and to centralise all the controls and quality inspections at the factory. We have a method of handling and freezing to keep the product fresh without using preservatives.

"Many competitors claim that they are able to also achieve the same process as us, but to date they have not been able to replicate our methodology. We maintain the edge in the industry with our unique method and process without hurting the taste and texture.

"This translates to better product management, and it is an attractive point of consideration for our franchisees as the cost of investment in an outlet is much lower versus

First Love
PATISSERIE

a traditional outlet. We provide a more effective and efficient business model that allows us to be different from our competitors.

"Moving forward, our team will continue to look at other aspects that will allow us to be stay ahead of our competitors."

How do you keep track of changing consumer preference and behaviour that could impact your brand?

"Consumer preferences are always changing. It's tough to anticipate and so we try to keep close to trends in the market. Through our strong R&D system, we are able to launch new products the moment we see an uptick in certain directions. There is no other way to find out but to observe closely.

"We have a policy which is to 'keep your friend close, the enemy even closer'. Through this, we keep learning from our competitors, evaluating their strategies and improving ours."

How has Covid-19 impacted your business and how did you react? Has Covid opened up new opportunities for you?

"In the beginning, the impact was so great that when all the malls in Indonesia were closed, we were forced to close all our outlets temporarily. Revenues were impacted, our distributors and B2B customers couldn't honour their orders and payments. By God's grace and support from our employees, we were able to weather the onslaught and still stand strong.

"When the domestic market was closed, we strengthened our exports to the international market. While the rest of the world also faced similar difficulties, our prior polices to maintain cash reserves and continued R&D allowed us to come out on top of it.

"The pandemic also gave us an opportunity to break out and start a small bakery project we had not been able to allocate time for. We believe that in the midst of difficulties, we have to continue to invest in the market.

"Another strength that was more prominent during this time was that our lean manufacturing structure allowed us to be able to make critical adjustments while not compromising on production and quality."

Can your brand stretch and extend into other segments? Any plans?

"We have been preparing to increase our capacity so that we can broaden our product lines. We also give support to many new online entrepreneurs by providing them with consulting services for the building of their own brands.

First Love
PATISSERIE

This in turn allows us to fill up our outstanding production capacity which would have otherwise gone to waste."

Where do you see your brand in five to ten years' time, in terms of business offer, geography, target groups?

"By standing by our company values, we believe that we will be able to push our brand and products to more international markets.

"We aim to continue to build trust in our customers by delivering consistent products with quality and integrity. Poor market conditions should not be a reason to sacrifice the quality of what we deliver.

"We are now undergoing a rebranding exercise, focusing more on our roots by diving deeper into Peranakan culture. We will be widening our menu and creating more product lines. To refresh the brand, we will be launching more mille crepes that are based off our traditional cakes but with a modern twist.

On top of this, we are already in the midst of moving into China and aim to first deliver our products to existing vendors followed by brand entry shortly after. If we are able to obtain suitable funding and work effectively with our partners, we hope to see our brand in more Southeast Asian markets and potentially some European cities."

LESSONS FROM COVID

- **Tap into culture for your brand positioning to make it more relevant and unique.**

- **When physical touchpoints are no longer possible, pivot towards delivery.**

- **Have a global mindset – what's impossible in one market may be possible in another.**

SO YOU WANT TO START A BRAND? #6

Brand Extension

WHEN YOU CAME UP with the idea for your startup, naturally you didn't just think about how to make it relevant, be different from the competition and consistent across all touchpoints, right? You also looked at the segment you're moving into. I know the brands in this book did.

Does it have potential? Will it grow? Are there any global trends (health, digital, convenience, personalisation, experiences) that will make the segment – and your brand with it – grow?

Often it is quite easy to see. Cigarettes and full-sugar carbonated soft drinks, for example, probably won't have much of a future. Think about government regulations and changing consumer behaviour.

But sometimes it's harder to spot: Is that a sunrise or a sunset on the horizon? Will this industry grow or die? In such cases, it's probably a good idea not to be too narrow in your brand positioning. Don't say you're selling carbonated soft drinks – sell refreshment. Then when the time comes, you can extend the brand into juices or water. Don't say you're selling internal combustion engine cars – sell mobility. Then you can move into e-mobility, hydrogen or any other ways that can bring the vehicle from A to B.

Look at it from a consumer perspective: Which need are you fulfilling? That's what you're offering, not the specific way you're meeting that need today.

Anybody Say Pizza?

GOPIZZA

KOREA

GoPizza is a new concept of pizza – fast pizza for single pax. Having started as a small food truck in Korea in 2016, the brand has grown explosively. In 2021, it opened its 100th global store in Suntec City, Singapore, serving its hallmark oval pizzas.

I first met Jay Lim just over ten years ago when he was an exchange student at SMU and attended my class. Even then, I noticed some sort of spark, some determination to make something happen. Later, at Audi Korea, I hired him to be part of the marketing department, where he excelled with attention to detail and people skills.

A year or two later, my head of events Hannah said to me: "Jay now has a food truck. Shall we try him out for the next concert we host?"

At the time, we brought global stars to Korea under the umbrella of Audi Live, mostly aimed at a younger demographic. From Bruno Mars to Pharrell Williams, we somehow managed to get the biggest stars of the time to perform in Seoul – and we combined it with a promotion for a car like the young Audi A1.

One of the ideas was to have food trucks of the hottest food brands in Korea outside the concert hall and offer samples for free. But Jay's brand was already gaining popularity and his truck was booked that day.

His growth since then has been phenomenal – based on a good understanding of differentiation, from the unusual format of the pizza to the need for brick-and-mortar outlets even during the pandemic.

Knowing Jay, the best is yet to come.

Interviewee
Jay Lim, Founder & CEO

GOPIZA

Share with us about the beginnings of your brand. What was the gap and opportunity you saw in the market?

"I'm an avid fan of McDonald's because of its price, convenience, and standardised offerings. Many people consider pizzas and hamburgers similar types of food, at least in Korea. But the consumer behaviours around these two foods are completely different.

"For example, pizza is at least two to four times more expensive than hamburgers, almost ten times slower, and so big that people always have to share.

"I thought buying a pizza from McDonald's would solve all those problems and probably would create a big market of people like me. Since McDonald's didn't sell pizza, I might as well make a pizza version of McDonald's."

Did you recognise a trend that you could tap into?

"Firstly, single-person households were increasing rapidly, from less than 20% to almost 40% within just ten years. But the difference was more than just the 20% growth per se; single-person households were becoming the 'majority', the norm.

"Secondly, pizza was becoming a commodity in Asia. It used to be a 'special' dish from the West and people were fine with paying more than $20 or $30 for a pizza. But now that 30 years had passed since its initial introduction in the market, people couldn't justify the price point."

How do you differentiate your brand from other players in your segment?

"We are the one and only brand that specialises in 'personal-sized pizzas' and hence we have the lowest price point (starting at $4.50, while the cheapest option in the pizza market starts at $6).

"We use real fire ovens that give our pizza the unique artisanal look and taste. And this end product stems from our innovative pizza operations technology."

How would you define your target group?

"Demographically, single-household consumers in the 15–34 age group. Our customers tend to have a more Westernised palate – enough to eat pizza more than once a week – and aren't used to sharing food (unlike earlier generations of Koreans, or Asians in general)."

When building your brand, what was the biggest hurdle you faced and how did you overcome it?

"When you are not a big brand, you have nothing to begin with. No brand awareness, no budget, no marketer, no

channel, nothing whatsoever. It was most difficult for me to know where to start because I only had experiences in marketing for big brands.

"That's why it's important to start small, by capturing whatever early customer groups you can.

"I started from one food truck and we grew to a $20-million revenue company in four years – and the branding started from the first customers who had our pizza. Since then, we've made everything better – price point, pizza shape, brand design – but the core ideas and USPs are exactly the same.

"It was difficult – but very important – to maintain that initial model while improving as a brand. You have to know what to keep and what to let go."

One way to create something new is to disrupt convention. What are you disrupting and how?

"Operations. We built everything from scratch. From dough, to toppings, to baking, to serving. Once you crack what people like in an F&B business, it all comes down to operations because it's a money-pinching business and we have 90 franchisees whose lives depend on our stores, quite literally.

"We adopted food engineering, mechanical engineering, Artificial Intelligence (AI), and even robotics to make personal pies in under 5 minutes just by one person. Without solving the operational barrier, it is quite impossible to make a profit from a personal-sized pizza restaurant business.

"Also, our oval pizza shape! It's disruptive on the first look. We wanted to send the message that it's not just a smaller version of the traditional pizza, it's a completely new product.

"We had hard time convincing customers of our oval pizza, and many times we were tempted to go back to a round shape. But we pushed even further and made our logo an oval shape.

"Now our pizza shape has completely settled down in the market, and whenever customers see an oval-shaped pizza, they think of GOPIZZA. I think we have successfully communicated our disruptive business model to customers through our unique shape."

How do you keep track of changing consumer preference and behaviour that could impact your brand?

"The increase in single-person households and pizza becoming a commodity combined have reshaped the pizza industry in Korea. It rapidly shrank to almost half within five years, while the frozen-pizza market grew bigger in the same period.

GOPIZZA

"We figured it's not that people started liking frozen pizza more – rather, consumers were looking for a cheaper, more casual, more convenient type of pizza.

"I think GOPIZZA nailed it reading the inner motive of consumer behaviours. For any data collection or research we do, we focus on consumers' underlying needs and the long-term effect of these needs. We don't decide on a strategy based on passing trends, though we do make use of those trends in marketing campaigns that last less than six months."

How has Covid-19 impacted your business and how did you react? Has Covid opened up new opportunities for you?

"For offline franchise businesses, Covid hit badly, but we still managed to grow more than 500% over the last two years. We have adopted delivery quickly and broadly, hence shifting our main channel of sales from dine-in to delivery (from 30% pre-Covid to 70% currently).

"But one thing I focused on was *not* to open ghost/cloud kitchen stores that *only* focus on deliveries, because I believe there is no future for those brands after Covid. They are not building a brand – as a matter of fact, most of them don't even have a brand. They just exist in the realm of delivery apps and are treated like commodities. When people stop using or use less of the apps, these brands stop to exist altogether.

"So all of our stores have a great presence in terms of location, exterior and interior design, and have at least 15–20 dining spaces.

"It was very hard to convince franchisees and investors to keep opening dine-in stores during Covid, but we managed to open more than 100 globally. Now that the pandemic is ending, our dine-in sales are up to 40% already, and we believe next year it will be more than 50%.

"Now, GOPIZZA is almost the only option when you want to dine out at a pizza shop, at least in Korea.

"We believe our philosophy in creating brand experiences in a physical environment while making kitchens as small as possible through various technologies will be the future of many F&B companies, especially after Covid.

"One good I can squeeze out from the pandemic is that since we specialise in single-person dining (or 'no-sharing' dining), I think people became more keen on the idea of personal pizzas during this period of 'safe distancing'."

Can your brand stretch and extend into other segments?

"As an F&B brand, we will probably only focus on making GOPIZZA the most successful global pizza brand, but our tech arm has plans to extend our kitchen technology (especially vision-based AI and robotics) to other pizza kitchens and similar F&B restaurant kitchens."

GOPIZZ

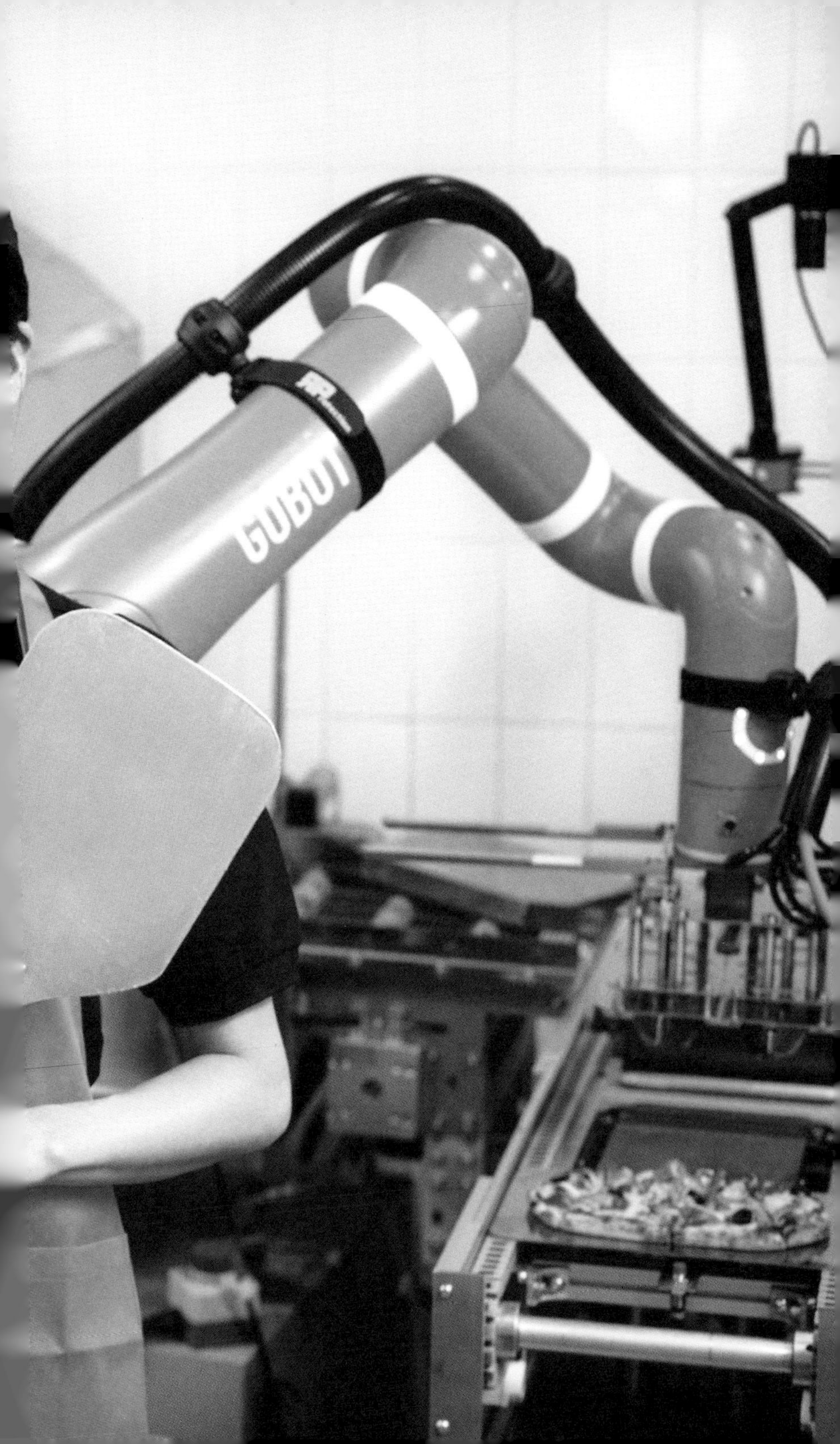
GUBOT

Where do you see your brand in five to ten years' time, in terms of business offer, geography, target groups?

"In ten years, we plan to have 10,000 stores globally, mostly in Asia. I hope that when people think of pizza, the first things that come to minds are: low price, quick service speed, and single-person servings – just like what you would expect from any other fast-food chain.

"And we will try our best to symbolise that change with our oval-shaped personal pizzas."

LESSONS FROM COVID

- **Be prepared to do delivery when physical outlets are temporarily unavailable.**
- **Keep in mind that delivery platforms make it harder for you to differentiate; keep as many physical touchpoints as you can to support the brand.**
- **Stick with your original concept and differentiator even when there is pressure to conform. It will benefit you in the long run.**

SO YOU WANT TO START A BRAND? #7

It's All About People

AT THE BEGINNING, it's all about you, the founder. You will be the face of the brand, and consumers will look to you to understand what the brand is all about.

That means you need to be aware of how you present yourself, how you look, dress, speak. Your personal social media channels will be synonymous with the brand's, and you will be asked to present and explain your brand, not just in internal presentations to investors and potential partners, also in public, in podcasts, TV interviews, newspaper write-ups.

Unless you're a natural, it would be a good idea to invest in a bit of media training, either online or, even better, with a coach. Often we're not aware of how we sit, stand, the faces we make and the words we use.

For example, in a client presentation in one of my branding classes, one of the presenters addressed the client as "you guys" more than seven times. This would be OK in a university environment, and this specific client was nice, but in a professional presentation, informal language can become a distraction or stumbling block. When I talked to the presenter about it, she wasn't aware that she used this so often. That's why you need a trainer to help you iron out the kinks.

Then, as your business grows, you will hire people to work with you. There will come a time when you can't do everything on your own and you will need support. Naturally, you will choose these people based on a number of considerations: their specific skillset, their experience, or because you know them and like them.

That's all fine, but make it a point to spend time with every new hire thinking about how they can represent the brand, because people are the most important touchpoint. Does their character, their attitude fit naturally with the brand positioning? Are they sending the right message about your brand when they speak to clients, investors and the public?

With a growing number of colleagues, the need for internal branding also grows. You have to make sure that they understand what the brand stands for and how that positioning needs to be expressed through their attitude and behaviour. It's not just about information – they also need to believe in the brand and its promise, be enthusiastic about the shared mission.

Towards that end, a handbook about the brand (digital or printed), together with regular listening sessions (where *you* listen to *them*), can be instructional and motivational, enabling them to send the same message that your marketing does – and be authentic and convincing when doing it.

SO YOU WANT TO START A BRAND? #8

Communicate

WHEN YOU START a brand, it becomes your life. You live, breathe and work the brand almost 24 hours of every day. And there's a temptation to think that everybody knows your brand, everybody cares about it – because of the huge role it plays in your life.

Unfortunately, that's not the case. Consumers get inundated with thousands of messages a day, most of which they don't care about because the products or services are not relevant to their lives.

You need to reach them and make them listen.

Reaching them is the easier part. Based on a good understanding of your target users and their media consumption habits, you choose the channels they are most likely to get their information from. If you're targeting hip 17-year-olds, TikTok is a must. For retirees, on the other hand, the printed version of the local newspaper may be more appropriate. Your targets won't go looking for you – you need to be where they are.

But keep in mind that a business TikTok, Instagram or LinkedIn channel doesn't work like a personal one, where you post an update once in a while and your friends give you likes or comments. Professionally, there's no such thing as organic reach. There are too many messages, there's too much competition for your post to be "automatically" seen.

So be prepared to put aside some seeding money for media. Just to make sure you even have a chance to be seen and heard.

The harder part is how you communicate. Naturally, each platform has its own rules, but in addition there are some global trends when it comes to advertising. The trend is: people don't like it. Or, to be specific: people don't like bad advertising. And most advertising is. Remember the last time you wanted to watch a YouTube video? Hovering with your cursor over the 'Skip ad' button in order to skip as soon as you could? Most people are like that.

In order to reach your target, you need to communicate in a way that makes them *want* to watch.

It could be that you're sharing an interesting and instructional piece of content – a cooking video, or a make-up tutorial, or an exclusive "behind the scenes" insider's look. Something entertaining, useful and share-worthy.

Or you could connect to a shared moment or event like New Year's Day, Christmas, Hari Raya, Deepavali,

Mother's Day or Earth Day – something that people are already paying attention to, in order to piggyback on that attention, to create a meaningful connection to the event that works for your brand.

A few years ago, when women in Saudi Arabia were first allowed to drive, my Hamburg agency showed me an idea to connect to that moment. It was called "Open Doors", and the endframe read: "It is time to open new doors. Audi welcomes the women of Saudi Arabia to the driver's seat." It was a bit of a risk to connect to a political moment, but with the help of colleagues in Dubai and Riyadh, we managed to produce an online video that went live just before the date and was well received around the world.

The video worked because we did not see it as an advertising opportunity to sell more cars; we just made a statement that positioned Audi as a progressive brand. That is the power of communication.

Conclusions

THANKS TO COVID...

It's interesting that despite looking at very different industries in very different markets, there are several key patterns emerging about how the Covid-19 pandemic has influenced and changed business – and how brands can actually benefit from that disruption.

Health

Naturally, at the tail-end of a global pandemic, health remains an important topic for consumers around the world, and any brand that can tap into that trend will benefit. From offering sanitisers (Bath & Bloom) to selling carefully curated products that are fresher and more healthy than the competition (Kurly), those that see consumers' needs and find a way to extend their brand to fulfil those have benefited from this trend.

Time

Yes, it is stressful for brands when suddenly they cannot operate and their world – like everybody's – is being turned upside down. But this extra time, because of a lock-down or other physical restrictions, can be put to good use. Many of the brands in this book have used it to reorganise their systems (VinFast) or even build up the brand and its positioning (BOVEM).

Delivery

When consumers couldn't go to brands, brands started to come to them and organised delivery to their homes. From food (Kurly, GOPIZZA) to sanitisers (Bath & Bloom), manscaping products (BOVEM) to career tools (Kinobi), e-commerce has benefited greatly from the pandemic and is likely here to stay.

But a word of caution comes from GOPIZZA's Jay Lim: It is harder to differentiate your brand on some delivery platform, and if you're not careful, you might be seen as a mere commodity. Try and keep some physical outlets to let consumers experience the brand – with all their senses.

International

All of the brands we looked at in this compilation, while originating in Asia, have global ambitions. Many have already moved into other markets in the region or internationally. This is not only a good growth strategy, it can also help overcome restrictions due to a pandemic or otherwise: not all markets will have the same closures or lockdowns at the same time, so if your physical connection to your customers isn't possible in one market, it may be working somewhere else. It always pays to keep a global perspective and be prepared to pivot at short notice.

Digital Communication

In a time where most people were hesitant to leave their house, many traditional communication channels were limited – out-of-home ads, even printed newspaper or magazine ads weren't able to reach as many customers as before. But consumption of digital channels – from news to streaming services, social media to forums – jumped up.

Almost all the brands I looked at used this opportunity (almost a necessity) to focus more than usual on digital communication – from dominating specific platforms like TikTok to using online influencers and building e-commerce platforms. And while more traditional channels like TV, cinema, print, press still have a role to play, online platforms will continue to be the go-to channels for most brands long after the pandemic is over.

ACKNOWLEDGEMENTS

IT'S HARD TO FIND up-and-coming brands, and I am grateful to the many collaborators, friends and former students who sent me long lists of what they saw as the next big brands in their respective markets:

Ng Yee Jian for Singapore, Masato Hori for Japan, Alex Lian for China, Handy Han for Korea, Max Mak for Hong Kong, Kanishk Kanakia for India, Suthisak Sucharittanonta for Thailand, Khiem Hoang for Vietnam, and so many others.

A big thank you to the brands in this book who participated, patiently answered questions and supplied pictures – all in a time of pandemic.

Finally, I am grateful as always to Melvin Neo and Justin Lau at Marshall Cavendish – for your belief in this idea.

ABOUT THE AUTHOR

JÖRG DIETZEL has worked with brands for over 30 years – running agencies in London, Berlin, Beijing and Singapore, heading the marketing department for Audi Korea 2013–16, and serving as global Head of Creative at Audi HQ 2017/18.

In 2005, he founded his own brand consultancy in Singapore and started teaching Strategic Brand Management and Advertising at Singapore Management University (SMU). Since 2019 he has also been teaching courses on Digital Outreach, Strategy and Branding for SMU Academy.

His favourite brands are Singapore, Singapore Airlines, Audi, Aesop, Monocle, Bynd Artisan, Dylan & Son, plus the many startups he's lucky to mentor.